DNA
AND
HEREDITY

Casey Rand

Heinemann
LIBRARY
Chicago, Illinois

www.heinemannraintree.com
Visit our website to find out
more information about
Heinemann-Raintree books.

To order:
☎ Phone 888-454-2279
🖳 Visit www.heinemannraintree.com
to browse our catalog and order online.

© 2011 Heinemann Library
an imprint of Capstone Global Library, LLC
Chicago, Illinois

Visit our website at www.heinemannraintree.com

Edited by Megan Cotugno and Andrew Farrow
Designed by Philippa Jenkins
Original illustrations © Capstone Global Library, Ltd.
Illustrated by KJA-artists.com
Picture research by Hannah Taylor
Production by Alison Parsons
Originated by Capstone Global Library, Ltd.
Printed and bound in China by Leo Paper Products Ltd.

14 13 12 11
10 9 8 7 6 5 4 3 2

Library of Congress Cataloging-in-Publication Data
Rand, Casey.
  DNA and heredity / Casey Rand.
    p. cm. -- (Investigating cells)
  Includes bibliographical references and index.
  ISBN 978-1-4329-3880-2 (hc)
 1. DNA--Juvenile literature. 2. Heredity, Human-
-Juvenile literature. 3. Cells--Juvenile literature. I.
Title.
  QP624.R36 2011
  572.8'6--dc22
                                2009049978

Acknowledgments
The author and publishers are grateful to the
following for permission to reproduce copyright
material: ©Alamy Images pp. 4 (©PHOTOTAKE/
Dennis Kunkel Microscopy, Inc.), 38 (©Image Source
Pink), 40 (©Photoshot Holdings, Ltd.); ©Corbis p.
23 (PhotoAlto/Odilon Dimier); ©Getty Images p. 39
(PPL Therapeutics via BWP Media); ©Istockphoto p.
34 (©Catherine Yeulet); ©Photolibrary pp. 5 (Jose
Luis Pelaez, Inc.), 13 (Grant Heilman Photography,
Inc.), 18 (Geophoto/Natalia Chervyakova), 25
(Dennis Kunkel), 31 (Dennis Kunkel), 32 (Pixtal), 41
(English Heritage), 42 (Walter H. Hodge); ©Science
Photo Library pp. 10 (Carl Goodman), 16 (A.
Barrington Brown), 17, 19 (Pasieka), 20 (Don W.
Fawcett), 21 (National Physical Laboratory ©Crown
Copyright), 29, 35 (Tek Image), 43 (Peter Menzel);
©shutterstock pp. 11 (©3DProfi), 22 (©Losevsky
Pavel), 36 (©Vava Vladimir Jovanovic), 37 (©Mogens
Trolle).

Cover photograph of a computer-generated DNA
double helix reproduced with the permission of
Getty Images (The Image Bank/SMC Images).

We would like to thank Michelle Raabe, Ph.D., for
her invaluable help in the preparation of this book.

Contents

Some words are printed in bold, **like this**. You can find out what they mean by looking in the glossary.

What Are DNA and Heredity?

Did you know that your entire body is made up of tiny units called cells? Cells are the building blocks of living things. Every part of you—your skin, muscles, hair, and even your eyes—is made up of cells.

But your hair is very different from your muscles. And your eyes are not like the skin on your arms. Even though every part of you is made up of cells, different cells have very different jobs from one another. They must perform their jobs so that the cells in your eyes can help you see, and the cells in your muscles can make you move.

But how do each of these cells know how to do their job? And where do they get this information? The answers are **DNA** and **heredity**.

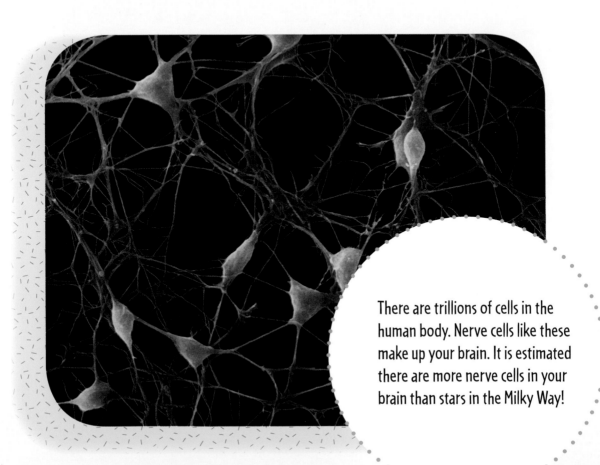

There are trillions of cells in the human body. Nerve cells like these make up your brain. It is estimated there are more nerve cells in your brain than stars in the Milky Way!

DNA

DNA is short for "deoxyribonucleic acid." It is the blueprint your cells use to determine how to do their job. DNA is like an instruction manual for your cells. It stores information just like the pages in a book. Your cells use this information to determine how to become part of your eyes or part of your ears, for example. Every tiny cell in your body contains a copy of the instruction book needed to form every part of you!

Heredity

DNA not only tells some of your cells how to become eye cells. It also tells these cells what color your eyes should be. Heredity is the passing of **traits**—things like eye color and height—from one generation to another. For instance, skin color is a trait that parents pass on to their children.

Many of our traits are determined by our DNA, which we receive from our parents.

What Is a Cell?

A cell is a tiny storage compartment. It holds the tools that perform the necessary functions that an **organism** (living thing) needs to live. Cells organize and store into one small space an abundance of tools and structures that an organism needs. Cells make up every living organism, including animals, plants, and even insects. Some organisms, such as human beings, are made up of trillions of cells. Other organisms are made up of just one cell!

Structures of the cell

Not all cells that make up human beings are the same. However, most cells in human beings hold the same structures, and these structures have the same job in all cells. For instance, the **mitochondrion** is known as the "powerhouse" of the cell. Its job is to help turn the food we eat into energy for the rest of the cell. The cell has many structures that need this energy to do their jobs. You can see some of these structures in the picture on page 7.

Proteins

Making **proteins** is one important function of the cell. Proteins are tools that help the cell function. Proteins give the cell shape, enable cells to communicate and move, and have many other functions in the cell. **Ribosomes** are the protein-making factories of the cell.

The nucleus: command center of the cell

The **nucleus** is like the brain of the cell. It tells the cell what to do, where to go, and even how to look. The nucleus holds the cell's **DNA**. This DNA tells the cell how to make the proteins it needs to function. Every tiny cell carries an entire copy of the organism's DNA within its nucleus.

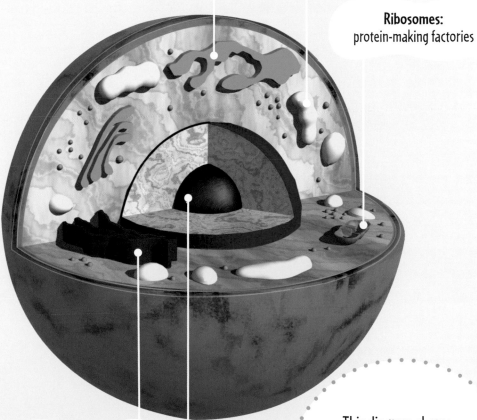

Golgi apparatus:
protein-packing plant

Mitochondrion:
powerhouse of cell

Ribosomes:
protein-making factories

Endoplasmic reticulum:
Cell's transportation system

Nucleus:
command center of the cell

This diagram shows the structures of a human cell and the jobs they do. Most human cells contain these same structures.

Tissues

Your eyes, ears, and nose are not made up of just one or two cells. Cells must work together to form these complex structures. Millions, or even billions, of cells combine to form groups called **tissues**. The cells of a tissue function together to form complex structures like bone, muscle, and skin. There are four major types of tissues in all human beings:

Muscle tissue
Whenever you run, jump, shake hands, or even blink, you are activating the cells of your muscle tissue. These cells work together to move your bones, so that your body can move.

Nerve tissue
Did you know that you owe your ability to think, speak, and feel to tiny cells? Cells of the nerve tissue work together to form your brain and spinal cord, as well as other nerve tissues.

Epithelial tissue
Epithelial cells form tight connections to protect your body from the outside environment, while keeping things like air and blood in the right location. Epithelial tissues form your skin, airways, and other linings.

Connective tissue
The cells of the connective tissue work as a team to hold all of the other tissues of the body in place. The connective tissue includes bone and ligaments, which are like strong rubber bands.

Making new cells

Cells are constantly dividing and making new cells. This is important both for growing and for replacing worn-out cells. Human beings start out as a single cell. This cell must divide over and over to form a baby and for the baby to grow. Cells of the major tissues get worn out and eventually need to be replaced with new cells.

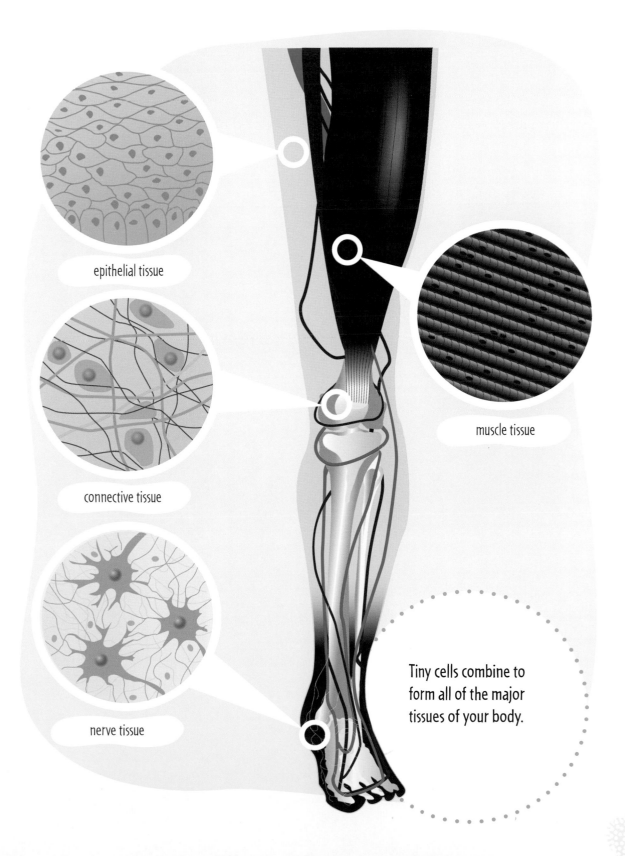

epithelial tissue

muscle tissue

connective tissue

nerve tissue

Tiny cells combine to form all of the major tissues of your body.

What Is DNA?

Every tiny cell in a human being carries a complicated plan in its **nucleus**. This plan is a blueprint capable of making a unique human being. Scientists call this plan **DNA**. But what language is this plan written in? And what exactly does it tell the cell?

The blueprint of life

DNA is a very complicated **molecule**. In a human, it acts as the blueprints, or instructions, that tell a cell how to build a whole new person. The DNA tells some cells how to become blood, some how to become hair, some how to become skin, and so on. DNA contains all of this information!

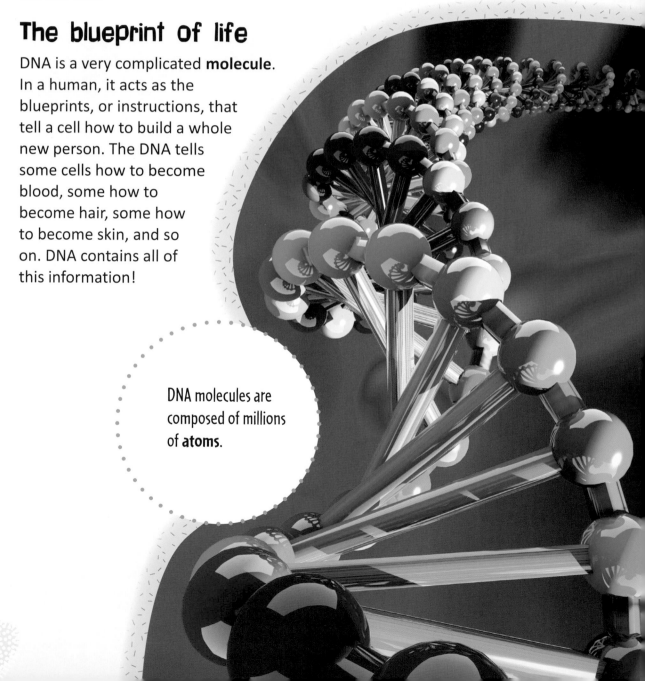

DNA molecules are composed of millions of **atoms**.

10

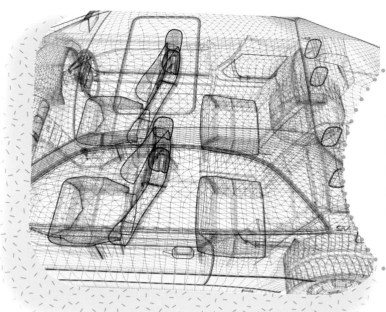

Blueprints contain instructions that reveal a detailed plan for building something, like this car. The DNA in cells is the blueprint for the way a plant or animal will be built.

Nucleotides

DNA is made up of four units that scientists call **nucleotides**. Scientists use the letters A, G, C, and T to represent these four units, or bases, of DNA. These bases are like the letters of the alphabet. You already know that letters of the alphabet combine to form sentences or stories. In a similar way, the nucleotides join together to form very long sentences or stories that the cell can read. These stories tell the cell how to create and maintain the **tissues** of the body.

Keep reading

If you started to read the nucleotides inside one little cell from your body at a rate of one nucleotide per second, you would be over 100 years old when you finished reading. And you would only finish in this time if you never stopped— even to sleep, eat, or use the bathroom! There are three billion nucleotides of DNA in every cell in your body.

The instructions of DNA: genes

Although there are billions of DNA nucleotides in every cell, not all of them are involved in making **proteins**. Only special parts of the DNA sequence, called **genes**, are used to make proteins. A gene is a set of instructions for making a specific protein. These proteins are the tools the cell uses to do its job.

Decoding the language of DNA

Remember that DNA is composed of four nucleotides that scientists refer to as A, G, C, and T. They form a language that the cell can read and use. Scientists have been able to decode one part of this language, but the other part remains mostly a mystery.

Exons

Exons are the part of the DNA that gives the cell instructions on how to make proteins. Many exons may join together to form one gene. These genes are expressed by the cell as proteins. This means the cell reads the instruction in the gene and uses them to build a protein. Just remember that **ex**ons are **ex**pressed as proteins.

Introns

But only about 2 percent of all DNA is made up of exons. The other 98 percent of the DNA is made up of **introns**. Scientists have not figured out exactly what introns do yet. They are still trying to decode this part of the language of DNA. Just remember that **in**trons are **in**-between genes.

UNDERSTANDING INTRONS AND EXONS

Only the exons of DNA are expressed as proteins. After the introns are cut out, the information is used to make proteins.

How many genes does it take?

Most complex **organisms** have a large number of genes. Humans have a lot of different parts, and making these parts requires a lot of instructions. But did you know there are many plants known to have even more genes than human beings?

ORGANISM	NUMBER OF GENES
Carsonella	182
yeast	6,000
fruit fly	13,000
human	25,000
flower	26,000
rice	60,000

The fruit fly has 13,000 genes.

What Does DNA Look Like?

We have learned that **DNA** is composed of long chains of the **nucleotides** A, G, C, and T. These chains are organized into alternating stretches of **exons** and **introns**. But how is a long chain of nucleotides held together? And how does such a long sequence fit inside the tiny **nucleus** of the cell? DNA must be organized very precisely to make sure it can fit in its tiny home, the cell nucleus.

The backbone of DNA

DNA nucleotides are held together by what scientists call a sugar-phosphate backbone. This backbone is sort of like a strong rope. The rope holds the nucleotides of DNA together so that long sequences of DNA can be formed. These long sequences of DNA are called DNA **molecules**.

The double helix

In most **organisms**, DNA molecules are found in matching pairs. Every molecule of DNA is attached to a matching molecule of DNA that runs in the opposite direction. The pair is held tightly together by bonds found between the two molecules. These bonds form what looks like rungs on a ladder. The rungs of the ladder are made only between certain bases. A always pairs with T, and C always pairs with G.

These ladders are twisted to form a helix, which looks kind of like a spiral staircase. This structure of DNA is called the **double helix**.

DNA, DNA, and more DNA

If you stretched out the DNA from every cell in your body into a straight line, it would be long enough to wrap around Earth over one million times!

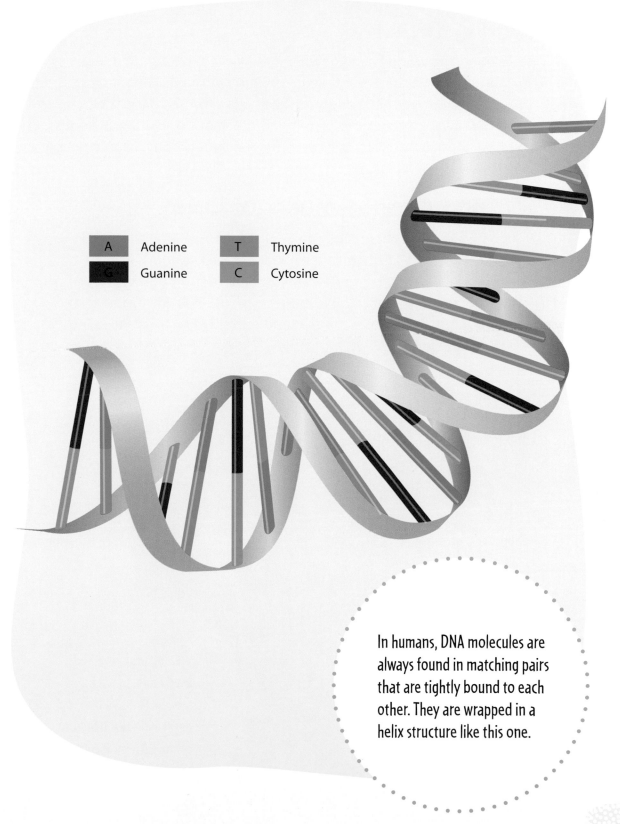

| A | Adenine | T | Thymine |
| G | Guanine | C | Cytosine |

In humans, DNA molecules are always found in matching pairs that are tightly bound to each other. They are wrapped in a helix structure like this one.

Discovering DNA

Scientists around the world have known about DNA for a long time. A Swiss scientist isolated DNA for the first time in 1869. A German scientist figured out what DNA was made out of just a few decades later. In the 1940s, a U.S. scientist proved that DNA carries **genetic** information (information relating to **genes**). But the most important and exciting discovery of all may have been determining the structure of DNA.

Watson and Crick: a model of DNA

The U.S. scientist James Watson and the English scientist Francis Crick worked together in the 1950s. They used ball and stick models, like the one in the picture below, to try to determine the structure of DNA. Watson and Crick built many different models, but they could not determine the correct model until they got some important help from scientist Rosalind Franklin (see box on page 17).

Watson and Crick used ball and stick models like this one to determine the structure of the DNA molecule.

Scientist Spotlight

Rosalind Franklin

A technique called X-ray diffraction allows photographs to be taken of very tiny images that are too small to be seen by regular photography. Rosalind Franklin (1920–1958) was an English scientist who, in the 1950s, used this method to take the famous photographs that helped determine the structure of DNA.

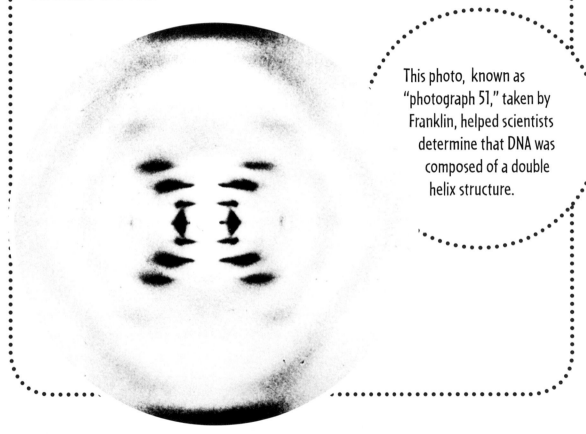

This photo, known as "photograph 51," taken by Franklin, helped scientists determine that DNA was composed of a double helix structure.

Teamwork

When Watson saw "photograph 51" taken by Franklin, his heart began to race and he became very excited. Watson knew that the fuzzy X-pattern he could see in the photograph indicated that DNA was a helix. This was new and exciting information to Watson and Crick. With this knowledge, they began a new model, and together they proved that DNA was a double helix. The combined expertise of Franklin, Watson, and Crick had finally solved the puzzle of DNA structure.

Chromosomes

In each cell, there are over three billion nucleotides of DNA sequence! How do the tiny cells hold so much DNA? DNA is organized and packaged into something called **chromosomes**. Chromosomes are structures that use **proteins** to contain and organize DNA. The DNA is wrapped around proteins like thread on a spool. Each chromosome can hold hundreds or even thousands of genes.

Chromosomes can be thought of like books used to organize the DNA library. Human beings contain 46 chromosomes in their cells. These chromosomes are stored in the cell nucleus. It is like each cell has a library, called the nucleus, with 46 books, called chromosomes. Each gene is like a chapter in a book that gives the cell instructions on how to make a particular protein. Each chromosome contains many of these chapters. This library contains all of the information needed to make every part of a human being.

Two copies is better than one

Human cells have two different copies of DNA. We receive one copy of DNA from our mother, and one copy from our father. Chromosomes are found in pairs. We have 46 chromosomes, so we have 23 pairs. In each pair one chromosome came from our mother and one came from our father.

ORGANISM	NUMBER OF CHROMOSOMES
mosquito	6
porcupine	34
human beings	46
gorilla	48
camel	70
dog	78
king crab	208
butterfly	380

This king crab has almost five times as many chromosomes as a human!

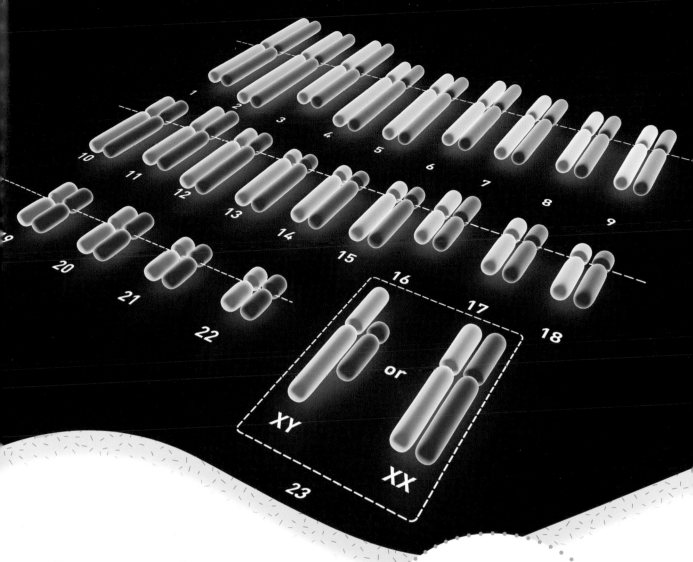

Boy or girl?

There are two special chromosomes that determine whether a new baby is a boy or a girl. These are called the sex chromosomes. The two sex chromosomes are the X chromosome and the Y chromosome. Girls normally have two X chromosomes, while boys normally have one X chromosome and one Y chromosome.

Humans have two copies of each chromosome for numbers 1 to 22. Then they have either two X chromosomes or an X and a Y chromosome.

Unraveling the mysteries of DNA

When DNA was first discovered by scientists, it was a big mystery. The small size of DNA made learning about this new substance very difficult. It is estimated that you could fit one million threads of DNA across the period at the end of this sentence. However, new technology has rapidly increased our knowledge about DNA in recent years (see below).

Science tools: the electron microscope

Scientists need powerful microscopes to be able to see DNA. The ability to see DNA came with the discovery of the electron microscope, which uses beams of electrons to magnify objects up to one million times their actual size. If you could look at an average-sized ant through an electron microscope with this much power, it would appear to be almost 5 kilometers (over 3 miles) long. That is one big, scary ant! But this is how much magnification scientists need just to be able to see DNA.

Electron microscopes today can magnify objects up to one million times their normal size, making strands of DNA visible for study by scientists.

Reading the code: the Human Genome Project

Although the structure of DNA was determined over 60 years ago, scientists knew very little about what DNA actually said until very recently. The **genome** is the entire DNA sequence, both exons and introns, of an organism. The Human Genome Project was a massive project begun with the goal of determining the entire human genome. The project took over 13 years, but in 2003 scientists revealed that the project had finally uncovered the entire human genome.

Some of the first electron microscopes, such as this one built in 1933, were only capable of magnifying objects to about 400 times their real size.

Big-money science

The Human Genome Project was coordinated mostly by the United States, but with labs working throughout the world. The project was estimated to cost over $3 billion. That's about $1 for every one of the over three billion nucleotides in the human genome.

How Do We Get Our DNA?

When a new life is started, whether it is a new plant, animal, or human being, **DNA** does not just magically appear. So, where does our DNA come from? And how does it get into the cells of a new **organism**?

From parents to children

The cells that become a new organism get their DNA from the parents of the new organism. In the case of human beings, a father supplies half of a new baby's DNA. The other half comes from the baby's mother. Remember that we have two copies of each of the 23 **chromosomes**. One copy comes from each of our parents. So, you have half the same DNA as your mother, and half the same DNA as your father.

The DNA that we have is not random. We inherit our DNA from our parents.

Traits

Many times family members look very similar to each other. They have similar **traits**. For instance, you may be tall like your father or have red hair like your mother. Or maybe you have green eyes that look just like one of your grandparents. These things are all traits.

Heredity

Why is it that families have similar traits? The answer is **heredity**. As we have seen, heredity is the passing of traits, like height or hair and eye color, from one generation to the next. When a child has a trait similar to one of his or her parents, that trait is said to be **inherited**. This means it was passed down from parent to child.

Not all of your traits are inherited. Sometimes the DNA from a baby's father and mother mixes together to form new traits in the baby.

The DNA inherited from the parents determines what color eyes a person will have.

Reproduction

For a new baby to be made, DNA from the parents has to be combined. This combination of parental DNA creates a new cell that has all of the instructions it needs to form a new baby. This process of combining DNA from parent organisms to form a new organism is known as **reproduction**.

In order for reproduction to occur, organisms have specialized cells called **sex cells**. These sex cells are responsible for bringing together the DNA from parent organisms so that a new life can begin.

Ovaries and eggs

In humans and many animals, the female sex cells are called **eggs**, and they are stored in the ovaries. The ovaries are egg-making and egg-storage facilities. A human female has nearly one million oocytes, which later turn into eggs, in each of her ovaries when she is born! Just like the other cells of the body, the egg contains a **nucleus** with DNA.

Testicles and sperm

The male sex cells are called **sperm**. The testicles are sperm-making and sperm-storage facilities. Every day the average adult male produces over 300 million new sperm! A fully developed sperm cell resembles a tadpole, but is much smaller. The head of the sperm cell contains DNA. The tail of the sperm helps the sperm swim to meet the egg.

Big and Small

The largest cell in the human body is the egg. The smallest is the sperm.

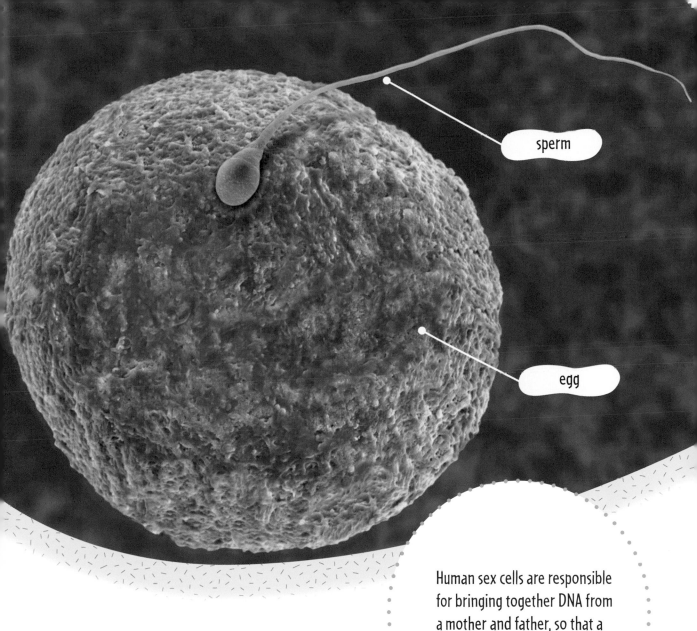

sperm

egg

Human sex cells are responsible for bringing together DNA from a mother and father, so that a new human can be formed.

Sperm and egg combine

During sexual intercourse, sperm is deposited in the female and swims to meet the egg. For reproduction to occur, a sperm and egg must unite. This is called **fertilization**. When the sperm and egg unite, the DNA from both father and mother are joined. The egg now has all of the DNA it needs to create a whole new individual.

Dividing DNA

For a new organism to form correctly, it needs to receive the right amount of DNA from each parent. The new organism needs to get copies of exactly half of its mother's DNA and exactly half of its father's DNA.

DNA in the sperm and egg

The sperm and egg are specialized for their job of making new babies. These cells contain only one copy of an organism's DNA—not two copies, like other cells. In humans the sperm and egg each have only half the normal amount of DNA (23 chromosomes). When the sperm and egg combine, the new cell has the normal number of chromosomes (46). This is the amount of DNA the cell needs to form a new organism. But how do these cells end up with only half of the normal amount of DNA?

Meiosis: dividing of chromosomes

The special process the body uses to form sperm and eggs with only 23 chromosomes (half the normal number of chromosomes) is called **meiosis**. Each time a cell goes through meiosis, it produces four new cells, each with only one copy of DNA. This is the amount of chromosomes the cells need to become a sperm or egg.

You can follow along in the picture to the right to see how meiosis works for a sperm cell. The picture shows only the two copies of chromosome 1, which are called 1A and 1B.

Unequal dividing

Sometimes meiosis does not work quite right, and a sperm or egg will have too many or too few chromosomes. This is very bad for the cells that will form a new baby. Even one extra or missing chromosome can cause disease or even death.

The three steps of meiosis are used to create four sperm cells with the correct amount of DNA for reproduction to occur.

STEP 1
DNA replication.
In this step, the cell makes a second copy of both chromosome 1A and chromosome 1B.

STEP 2
Cell division 1.
This step divides chromosome 1A and chromosome 1B into two new cells.

STEP 3
Cell division 2.
This step divides the new copies of each chromosome made in step 1 into two new cells.

How Do Our Cells Use DNA?

When **fertilization** occurs, the **egg** cell has all of the **DNA** it needs to form a new, unique person. This cell will divide over and over again to make new cells. These new cells will divide over and over again as well. All of these new cells contain the same DNA as the original fertilized egg.

However, not all of these cells will look and function the same. Some cells will become part of the heart, some will become part of the brain, some will become part of the blood, and so on.

Multiplying cells

One cell becomes many through a process called **replication**. Replication is the division of one cell into two. Part of replication is **mitosis**. In mitosis the **nucleus** makes a copy of its DNA. That way, after replication, each new cell can have one full copy of DNA.

Through cellular replication one cell can become many. Not all cells will become the same type. Most **organisms** need many different types of cells.

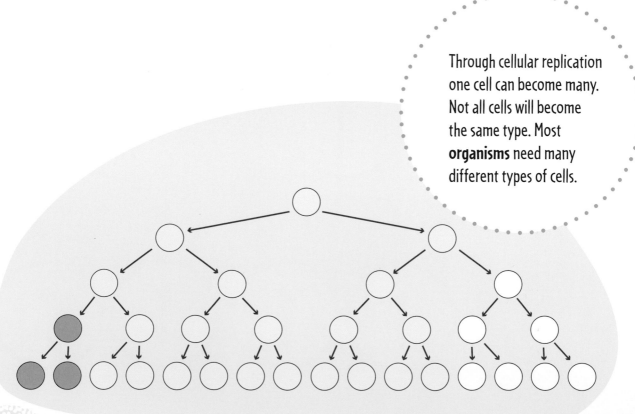

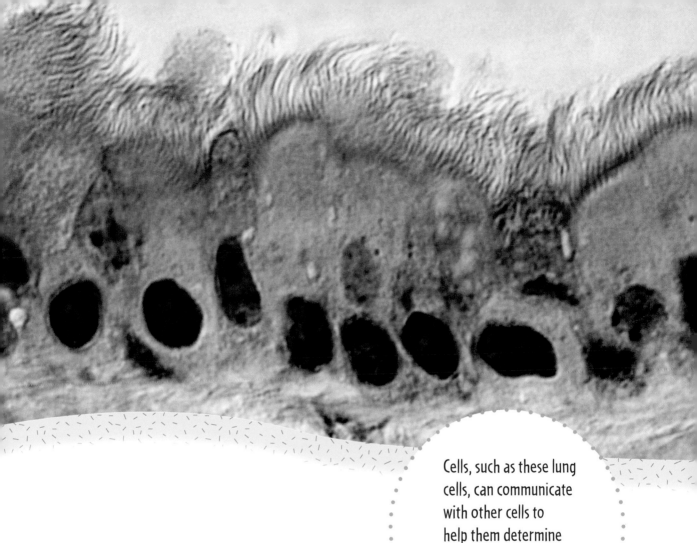

Cells, such as these lung cells, can communicate with other cells to help them determine what job they need to perform.

Cell communication

Each cell in your body has the same DNA. But each cell has a unique job. Each job requires the cell to use specific parts of its DNA. In order for a cell to know what its job is, it communicates with the cells around it.

Cells can communicate directly with other cells around them. Cells can even send out signals to cells that are farther away. Cells can tell other cells where they are located and what job they have. This helps cells to know what part of the DNA they need to use to become the kinds of cells they will become. For example, this is how cells in the lungs know to become lung cells, and how cells in the muscle know to become muscle cells.

Proteins: the tools of the cell

Once the cell determines what its job is, it needs to create the right tools to carry out its job. The tools a cell uses are made mainly of **proteins**. The cell already has all of the information it needs to make these tools in its DNA.

From DNA to mRNA

Ribosomes are the cell's protein-making factories. These are found outside of the nucleus in the cell. DNA is found inside the nucleus. So the cell uses a special messenger service called messenger **ribonucleic acid** (m**RNA**) to deliver the instructions of DNA in the nucleus to the protein factories outside the nucleus.

When the cell determines it needs a certain protein, it figures out where the instructions are in the DNA for making that protein. The cell then uses a specific **enzyme** to encourage a chemical reaction in the body. This copies a **gene** in the DNA into an mRNA **molecule**. This mRNA copy can move outside the cell nucleus to deliver the instructions to the ribosomes.

Making proteins

When an mRNA molecule arrives at a ribosome, the ribosome reads the instructions in the mRNA and makes the protein that the cell needs. Now the cell has the tools it needs to perform its job:

- DNA: instructions for making the cell's tools

- mRNA: the messenger that delivers the instructions

- ribosome: the factory that reads the instructions and makes the tools

- proteins: tools the cell uses to perform its job.

Muscle cells use a protein tool called myosin, which helps the muscle cell become capable of making you move and flex your muscles. When the cell nucleus decides more myosin is needed, it makes a copy of the DNA instructions for myosin and sends them to the ribosome (pictured here) for myosin to be made.

What Are the Laws of Heredity?

In the mid-1800s, a scientist from Austria named Gregor Mendel wanted to know why certain **traits** seemed to be **inherited**, and what the rules were for this inheritance. Mendel did not know about **genes** or **chromosomes** at the time—although he did suspect that parents passed on traits to their children. Mendel used pea plants to determine how **heredity** worked. He became known as the father of genetics, which is the branch of science that deals with heredity.

Mendel worked with pea plants because they have simple **genetic** traits that are easy to identify and track.

Mendel's experiment

Pea plants have flowers. Some of the pea plants Mendel used had purple flowers, while others had white. This allowed Mendel to easily track the inheritance of flower color. Mendel used a method called **crossbreeding** to discover the laws of heredity. Mendel would **breed** (produce offspring) a pea plant using one purple-flowered pea plant and one white-flowered pea plant. Then Mendel would wait to see what color flowers the new pea plants would have.

Mendel discovered that when he bred purple pea plants with white pea plants, the results were always purple pea plants. However, when he bred these new purple pea plants together, sometimes a white pea plant would appear.

PATERNAL GENERATION

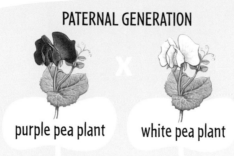

purple pea plant   X   white pea plant

Mendel used the color of pea plant flowers to help determine the Law of Segregation.

FIRST GENERATION OF OFFSPRING

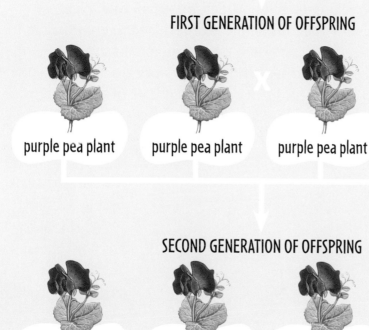

purple pea plant   purple pea plant   X   purple pea plant   purple pea plant

SECOND GENERATION OF OFFSPRING

purple pea plant   purple pea plant   purple pea plant   white pea plant

The Law of Segregation

This helped Mendel determine that each inherited trait is defined by a pair of genes. Each copy of the gene is called an **allele**. The two alleles are randomly separated in the **sperm** or **egg**, so that each sperm and egg contains only one allele of the pair. Offspring therefore inherit one allele from each parent when the sperm and egg unite.

Why Are We Different Or Similar?

Everyone is unique! None of us looks exactly the same. But in general human beings are all very similar. Certainly you are more similar to your classmates than you are to a mouse.

Variation in DNA among humans

The **DNA** sequence from one human to another is about 99 to 99.5 percent identical. But remember that the **genome** (an **organism's** total **genetic** material) is huge. Even a difference of 0.1 percent in the genome means we all have many differences in our DNA. Scientists have already found more than one million places where variations in human DNA can be identified. All of these differences in DNA sequence, varying from one person to another, are a major reason we are all unique.

No two people look exactly alike, but we all look similar.

Brothers and sisters

Each **sperm** or **egg** contains half of the DNA of the father or mother. However, each time a sperm or egg is made, it has a unique combination of DNA. The **chromosomes** mix and recombine differently in each cell. This is why brothers and sisters may look similar, but never exactly the same. Brothers and sisters are more genetically alike than unrelated people, but they still have a lot of differences.

DNA fingerprints

Sometimes the police can identify someone based on the unique pattern of his or her fingerprints. Now police can use "DNA fingerprinting." DNA fingerprinting is using the unique pattern of someone's DNA to identify him or her. No two people have exactly the same pattern of DNA sequence. DNA can be found in hair, skin, blood, or even saliva (spit).

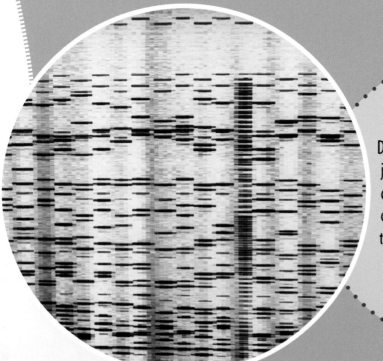

DNA fingerprints can be used just like regular fingerprints to determine who was at the scene of a crime, or to determine the true identity of a person.

We are not so different

Horses do not seem too much like cats. And dogs do not seem too much like spiders. Human beings definitely do not seem anything like starfish. However, all of these **species** (groups of the same type of living thing) have the same genetic material. That is, they all have DNA.

In fact, every known living organism on Earth has DNA. Humans have a lot of identical sequences with many of these animals, insects, and even plants. Sometimes DNA tells us that animals are more alike than they first appear. Have a look at the hyrax on page 37, for instance.

Eat, drink, sleep

We have already learned that much of how you look is determined by your DNA. However, DNA is not the only factor in determining how you look and who you are. The environment you are in influences who you are and how you develop. This includes what you eat, what you drink, how much sleep you get, and many other things. This is why it is so important to take good care of your body.

Your body and its millions of cells need rest to stay healthy and fight disease.

Nature versus nurture

Is DNA ("nature") more important to who you are and how you look? Or are your environment and experiences ("nurture") the biggest factor in determining these things? Many people call this the "nature versus nurture" argument. Although scientists are still not sure which influence is the biggest, or exactly what each determines, we know that both are a very big influence on who people are.

The hyrax is the closest living ancestor of the elephant. It shares over 90 percent of its DNA with the elephant, but it does not look like an elephant, use a trunk to drink, or make a trumpet noise.

Identical twins share nearly identical DNA.

Twins

Under normal circumstances, one sperm **fertilizes** one egg and one new baby develops. However, sometimes a female may become pregnant with two or more babies at once. This is a perfect opportunity for scientists to study the effects of nature and nurture on human beings.

Fraternal twins

Sometimes two different female eggs will be fertilized by two different sperm. These are called fraternal twins. Since each of these twins is formed from a different egg and a different sperm, they will each have a different combination of DNA. But they will share the same space in their mother's womb, and they will be exposed to the same environment during the pregnancy. Fraternal twins provide a great opportunity for study.

Identical twins

Identical twins have nearly identical DNA. They are both formed from the same egg and the same sperm. This happens when a fertilized egg divides and forms two different balls of cells, each of which will become a baby. Each of these balls of cells has the same combination of DNA. Like fraternal twins, they will also share the same environment in their mother's womb. That is why these twins will look so much alike and are so good for studying the effects of nature. When they are separated and grow up in different environments, identical twins can also be useful for studying the effects of nurture.

Clones

In 1996 a team of Scottish scientists produced a sheep named Dolly. She was the world's first cloned mammal. Cloning is when scientists create an organism with a DNA sequence identical to that of another organism. This kind of cloning is a very controversial topic, as it is not fully understood and sometimes has unexpected results.

Animal cloning has proved that the genetic material inside of our cells has all of the necessary instructions for building an entirely new organism. These five cloned piglets were born in 2002.

What Happens When DNA Changes?

During cell division and **DNA replication**, changes sometimes occur to DNA sequences. Sometimes changes occur in DNA sequences that lead to changes in how the cell makes **proteins**. This kind of change is known as a **mutation**.

Bad mutations

Many mutations are not good. Under normal circumstances, a cell makes proteins in a way that works well with how the cell functions. When a change occurs, this affects the ability of the cell to function in its normal way. Mutations of DNA sequence are known to cause many **genetic** diseases, such as hemophilia (a blood disease that affects blood clotting), and can even cause death.

Good mutations

Sometimes mutations in DNA sequences can be good, however. They can lead to changes in the function of the cell that may actually be beneficial to the survival of the cell or **organism**.

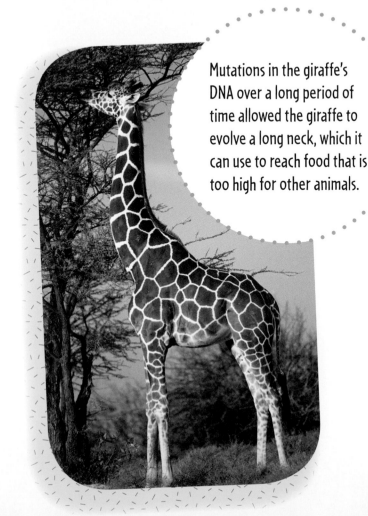

Mutations in the giraffe's DNA over a long period of time allowed the giraffe to evolve a long neck, which it can use to reach food that is too high for other animals.

If a DNA mutation leads to the survival of an organism, this mutation will likely be passed on to the next generation, which will also benefit. The process of evolution is based on these beneficial mutations. Evolution is when there are changes to a **genome** of a population over a series of generations.

Charles Darwin

English naturalist Charles Darwin (1809–1882) became famous in the 1800s for his theories on evolution and **natural selection**. He presented his theories in his book *Origin of Species* (1859). Darwin's theories were based on organisms slowly evolving through DNA mutation.

Darwin was the first person to present major evidence indicating that all life had evolved from a common ancestor (living thing that lived a long time ago).

Human-made genetic changes

As scientists have learned about DNA sequence and how to manipulate it, they have found ways to use DNA changes in beneficial ways. **Genetic engineering** is any method scientists use to make changes to **genes** to make them perform in a different way.

Genetic engineering of plants

Genetic engineering can be used to create new types of crops that will feed more people. There are two major types of genetic engineering in plants: **crossbreeding** and modern genetic manipulation.

Crossbreeding

In the method called crossbreeding, people **breed** closely related **species** of plant—for example, one type of apple tree that grows well in dry conditions and another type that grows giant apples. Farmers can breed these two plants and might create a new kind of tree that both grows well in dry conditions and grows giant apples.

Modern genetic manipulation

Scientists have recently developed the ability to introduce single genes into the genome of crops. This allows genes from any species to be introduced into crops.

Genetic engineering has made it possible to grow larger fruits that are also resistant to frost.

This baby suffers from a disease called SCID, or severe combined immunodeficiency, which makes it more likely to get a serious, life-threatening infection. Gene therapy offers new hope in treating SCID.

Gene therapy in humans

Many diseases are caused by genetic mutations. Gene therapy is a new method that allows doctors to insert a new, good gene in place of a mutated gene that is causing disease. This therapy does not always work. But it has been shown to help doctors treat some cancers, as well as **inherited** forms of deafness and blindness.

DNA and heredity in the future

With all of the new technology and information we are learning about DNA and **heredity** today, the future is going to be very exciting! Will we find new ways to treat disease, to slow aging, or to grow crops in the desert? These exciting discoveries will be up to young scientists like you in the years to come.

Glossary

allele single form of a gene, when multiple forms are possible

atom smallest unit of an element

breed to produce offspring through sexual reproduction

chromosome body in the nucleus of a cell that contains and organizes DNA

crossbreed process of breeding plants or animals with the intention of creating offspring that share the traits of both parent plants

deoxyribonucleic acid (DNA) nucleic acid that carries the genetic information in the cell and is capable of self-replication

double helix coiled structure of double-stranded DNA

egg female sex cell that is capable of combining with the male sperm to begin a new life

enzyme substance that encourages a chemical reaction in the body

exon sequence of DNA that codes information for protein synthesis, or is part of a gene

fertilization union of a male sperm and female egg

gene stretch of DNA located on a chromosome that tells a cell to make a specific protein

genetic relating to genes

genetic engineering direct manipulation of an organism's genome to change the way an organism functions

genome organism's total genetic material

heredity passing of traits from one generation to the next

inherit receive a characteristic from a parent through genes

intron segment of a gene situated between exons in the DNA that does not function in coding for protein synthesis

meiosis cell division in organisms that reduces the number of chromosomes in reproductive cells from two copies to one copy

mitochondrion (plural: mitochondria) structure in a cell that deals with producing energy

mitosis type of cell division that produces two identical cells

molecule group of atoms bonded together into the smallest unit of a substance

mutation change of the DNA sequence within a gene or chromosome

natural selection process by which plants and animals most suited for life in their environment will be most likely to continue to live and breed, while others die out

nucleotide basic unit of DNA

nucleus command center of the cell

organism individual form of life, such as a plant or animal

protein structure created by genes that helps the cells of the body specialize

replication copying of a cell's DNA and division of the cell into two cells, each with complete copies of the DNA

reproduction process by which organisms generate new individuals of the same kind

ribonucleic acid (RNA) base sequence that codes for protein synthesis and the transmission of genetic information

ribosome protein factory of a cell

sex cell sperm or egg; cell used in the process of reproduction

species living things that are the same type and can reproduce

sperm cell produced by the male reproductive system that is capable of fertilizing the female egg

tissue group of cells that function together to form complex structures in the body

trait inherited characteristic, such as eye or hair color

Find Out More

Books to read

Ballard, Carol. *Cells and Cell Function.* New York: Rosen, 2010.

de la Bedoyere, Camilla. *The Discovery of DNA*. Strongsville, Oh.: Gareth Stevens, 2006.

Hartman, Eve, and Wendy Meshbesher. *DNA and Heredity*. Chicago: Raintree, 2009.

Johnson, Rebecca L. *Amazing DNA*. Minneapolis: Millbrook, 2008.

Websites

"Cells Alive!"
www.cellsalive.com
This interactive website has lots of fun information about cells.

"DNA from the Beginning"
www.dnaftb.org
Explore lots of great images and animations to help you learn about DNA.

"Genetics: What Are Genes?"
www.sciencekidsathome.com/science_topics/genetics-a.html#more
This website has tons of information on genetics, written just for kids.

"NASA Kids' Club"
www.nasa.gov/audience/forkids/kidsclub/flash/index.html
This National Aeronautics and Space Administration (NASA) website is filled with fun science facts.

Become an expert

- Find out how many genes your favorite organisms have. For example, a human has 25,000 genes. Do you know how many genes a flower has?

- Learn more about the fascinating Rosalind Franklin, who took photographs using a technique called X-ray diffraction.

- Do you know how an electron microscope works? If not, go to your school or public library and research this powerful science tool.

- What is cloning? Learn more about this controversial topic.

- Read a book about Charles Darwin to discover who this naturalist was and what famous theories he proposed.

Index